# Pergamano

## STAMPING ON

## PARCHMENT PAPER

MARTHA OSPINA

LA RIVIÈRE
CREATIEVE UITGEVERS

# CONTENTS

*Pergamano® is the brand name under which
books, materials and tools for the creative hobby
Parchment Craft are marketed.*

2ᵗʰ Edition, 1998
© 1997 La Rivière, creatieve uitgevers, Baarn.

Editor: Anja Timmerman
Illustrations: Martha Ospina
Cover design: Studio Jan de Boer, Vianen
Design/Layout: Studio Imago, Amersfoort
Translation: Ellarik Services, Bilthoven

ISBN 90 384 1245 2
NUGI 440

# PREFACE

It is amazing how the creative hobby Parchment Craft
manages to keep on widening its boundaries!
When creative stamping on ordinary paper was booming
we noticed how the more creative people took the
initiative to experiment with stamping on parchment
paper. The results were so beautiful that we decided to
make this instruction book.
Thanks to the transparency of parchment paper, unique
leaded or stained glass window effects can be obtained.
The contour lines of the pattern are made in relief in a
leaden colour and the areas in between are coloured with
transparent Pergamano painting materials. The pattern w
stand out beautifully against background lighting.
You can make all sorts of things with Pergamano "leade
glass", for example window hangings, mobiles, Christma
decorations, folding cards and lamp shades. Not
everybody will be able to follow a course from a
Registered Pergamano Tutor, therefore I am convinced
that this book will provide all the necessary information.
In this instruction book you will find the basic technique
required, along with useful tips especially for stamping o
parchment paper. When I wrote my previous books, I wa
very happy to be able to count on Pergamano Tutors to
help me with the pieces of work, and this time Registere
Tutor Mieke Sprenger helped me; she has made all the
pieces of work in this workbook. I would like to take the
opportunity to thank Mieke again for her help and suppo
Thanks to Mieke and the constructive co-operation with
my editor, Anja Timmerman, I have been able to write
another beautiful Crea-Book. I wish you lots of fun with
creative stamping on parchment paper!

Martha Ospi

# 1. INTRODUCTION

The creative hobby Parchment Craft has many techniques. The most important ones are: tracing a pattern, embossing, perforating, cutting and painting.

With the transparent parchment paper you can make greetings cards, bookmarks, boxes, wall decorations, Christmas decorations, and even realistic flowers.

Instead of tracing a pattern, you can also stamp the pattern on to parchment paper.

Does the stamping on parchment paper have more to offer than stamping on white or coloured ordinary paper? Yes indeed! We will make use of the fact that parchment paper is opaque. It is thanks to this property we will be able to imitate the leaded (stained) glass window decorations. We can also combine the stamping with almost all of the existing Parchment Craft techniques as well as with other materials, for example cardboard passe-partouts to frame the pieces of work.

In the next few chapters we will show you step-by-step how it is all done.

Ready to go ahead?

We assume you are familiar with the basic principles of Parchment Craft.

Should this not be the case, then there are two ways to learn them:

1. You can learn them yourself with the help of the book Pergamano, Basic Techniques, (ISBN no. 90 384 1247 9)
2. You can follow a course with a Registered Pergamano Tutor. Write a letter to Marjo Arte B.V., P.O. Box 2288, 1180 EG Amstelveen, The Netherlands, and you will receive the address of a Registered Tutor in your neighbourhood.

# 2. MATERIALS AND TOOLS
*(Picture on page 3)*

The main materials and tools required for stamping on parchment paper are:

- **The Pergamano® stamps**
  The stamps consist of:
  – a synthetic block with indented sides for a good grip; the full-size picture of the stamp is visible on the top
  – underneath: a reddish rubber stamp on a layer of rubber to facilitate making a good and complete print.

The blocks of most rubber stamps are made from wood. The synthetic Pergamano® blocks have the advantage that they will not deform due to shrinking or humidity, but it is made to look like Beech wood. You can even hold the stamp under the tap, which makes it very easy to clean. The rubber stamps should be kept in a cool and dark place.

- **Ink pad**
  The ink pad consists of a plastic box with a cushion inside saturated with transparent or coloured stamping ink.
- **Embossing powder**
  Embossing powder can be sprinkled on a stamped design which is still wet, and will afterwards then melt when heated. The powder is usually sold in 20 gram plastic containers. For the "leaded glass" effect we used silver embossing powder, but it is also available in gold and other colours.
- **Pergamano® ruler for stamping**
  This is a set square, with two sides at right angles made from the same material as the synthetic blocks of the stamps. You will need this ruler to pin point the exact position you require your stamped impression.
- **Perga-Color felt tip pens**
  Perga-Color pens can be used to moisten the rubber stamp instead of the ink pad. If you wish to use them for this purpose, the pens should be new and full of ink, otherwise they will not moisten and colour the rubber stamp sufficiently. The Perga-Color pens are also particularly suitable for the colouring inside the 'leaded' areas.

- **A heating source**
  This could be an old toaster, a travel iron or ordinary iron (not being a steam iron) or a heating gun.

**Other materials:**
– Pergakit, transparent glue for 3-D projects
– Pergamano® eraser
– Pergamano® junior brush (light brown handle)
– embossing and perforating tools
– embossing pad
– Pergamano® parchment paper, 150 grams.

# 3. STAMPING

We will now make our first print. For this exercise we will use the Pergamano® stamp PS2 (tropical bird). First, set out everything you will need:

- Pergamano® stamp PS2 "Tropical Bird in Art Nouveau style"
- an ink pad filled with transparent ink
- silver coloured embossing powder
- a heating source; we chose a toaster
- Pergamano® parchment paper 150 gr./m², at least 10 x 10 cm
- a sheet of cardboard to work on
- a sheet of white paper to collect excess powder
- a cotton rag to dry off the stamp.

## 3.1 Printing
- place the parchment paper on a flat surface
- take the stamp in one hand and the ink pad in the other
- press the stamp against the ink pad a few times, making sure that the whole surface of the stamp is sufficiently moistened (picture 1)
- hold the stamp in both hands between your thumb and forefinger
- hold the stamp horizontally about 1 cm above the centre of the parchment paper; take care to place the stamp in the centre of the paper
- now make a print on the paper, press firmly without jiggling the stamp (picture 2)
- remove the stamp carefully from the parchment paper without making a sliding movement.

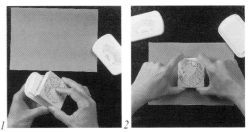

*1*  *2*

When transparent ink is used, the result will be very feint; however, as the print is wet, you should be able to see it properly.

If the pattern has not been printed completely:
a. check whether the surface you work on is completely flat
b. check whether the stamp had enough ink every-where
c. press a bit harder on the stamp

Repeat this exercise a few times to get the hang of making good prints.
Whilst the print is still wet, the embossing powder should be sprinkled on to the print. Do this as quickly as possible, because when the print has dried, the embossing powder will not adhere to it.

## 3.2 Applying embossing powder
- place the project in front of you and sprinkle a sufficient amount of embossing powder on to the wet print (picture 3). The print will be clearly visible as the grey powder will stick to the wet lines
- take the parchment paper in your hands, hold it

horizontally and shake it carefully to ensure that every line of the print is filled with powder

### 3.3 Recovery of excess powder

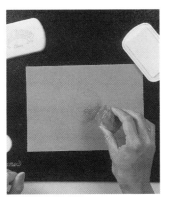

*3*

Put a sheet of ordinary white paper in front of you and make a centre fold.
Take your work and allow the excess embossing powder to fall on to the white paper (picture 4)
- let your project hang vertically and tap against it with your fingers to remove the remainder of the excess embossing powder
- pour the excess powder back into its container (picture 5).

*Attention:* embossing powder tends to stick to the paper in areas where you did not press the stamp. In order to be able to remove it properly, you will first of all have to tap well against the paper and furthermore you can remove the remainder of the unwanted powder with the brush part of the Pergamano® eraser.

*Another tip:* we advise you not to use your good Pergamano® brushes, because the slightest amount of embossing powder could ruin them.
Embossing powder can also stick to finger-marks! Hold your sheet of parchment paper only by the corners, as these usually will be removed when you finish off a project.

### 3.4 Cleaning of the stamp

Allow ample time to clean the stamp:
- hold it under a running tap
- clean it with a soft brush
- dry the stamp off with a cotton cloth or kitchen paper.

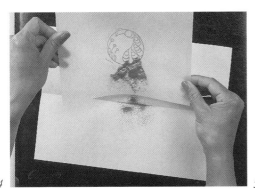

*4*

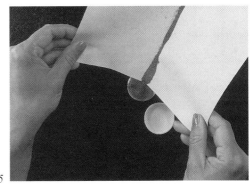

*5*

# 4. MELTING

Once heated, the embossing powder melts and will then stick to the parchment paper.

## 4.1 Using a heating gun.

It is recommended that you use a heating gun specifically designed for stamping. There are several types of heating guns, therefore we can only give general instructions.

– start at low temperature (if you can adjust the temperature), and direct the heating gun towards the stamp print
– hold the heating gun about 15 cm. away from your piece of work
– watch the powder start to melt
– if it does not melt, increase the temperature of the heating gun or bring it a bit closer to your piece of work

– experiment to discover the best position and temperature for the melting of the embossing powder.

Avoid unnecessary overheating of the parchment paper to prevent it from drying out.

Little stray dots of melted embossing powder may at first appear, but you can try to erase these with the Pergamano® eraser on a flat, hard surface.

## 4.2 Using a toaster

When using a toaster as your heat source for melting the embossing powder, do take care, as it is possible that a little of the embossing powder could drop into the toaster. You should then not use it for toasting bread anymore.

*Procedure:*

– turn on the toaster, if possible, at its highest temperature
– wait about a minute until the toaster has reached its temperature
– take your piece of work and hold it with the stamp face up, about 1 cm. above the toaster
– gently move your piece of work slowly over the openings of the toaster until all the powder lines have melted
– place your piece of work back on your table
– turn off the toaster.

9

The above procedure should take approximately one minute. To avoid fire, do not place your piece of work on the toaster, or walk away leaving your parchment paper near by. If your parchment paper does turn brown, the temperature has been set too high. Lower the temperature and/or hold the parchment paper higher above the toaster.

# 5. COLOURING

You will discover that the melted silver embossing powder lines that look like the thick grey lines of leaded glass window.

To colour the 'glass' area of the 'window', one can use various Pergamano® colouring products:
1. Perga-Color felt tip pens
2. Tinta inks
3. Perga-Liners
4. Pintura or Pinta-Perla paints (transparently painted)
5. a combination of the four above-mentioned products.

The Perga-Color felt tip pens are particularly suitable for simply colouring the piece of work (picture 7). As we mentioned in the introduction, we assume you are familiar with this particular painting technique.

The project shown in the picture is fitted into rings of passe-partout cardboard (see pattern no. 1) and has been coloured with Perga-Color number 6 and 12.

You can work with or without the Pergamano® brush, however, the result will be more beautiful if you do use a brush (picture 16).

7

### *Framing of the project*
This is how to make the passe-partout for this piece of work:
- choose passe-partout cardboard in a matching colour
- cut two equal rings with a hobby circle cutter
- cut the parchment piece of work in a circle with a diameter of 5 mm smaller than the passe-partout
- glue the piece of work and the passe-partout rings together with glue or thin double-sided adhesive tape
- make a little hole in the passe-partout with the single needle perforating tool for the hanging thread.

Hang your project against the light. Make two or more equal projects and interconnect them to make a sort of mobile.

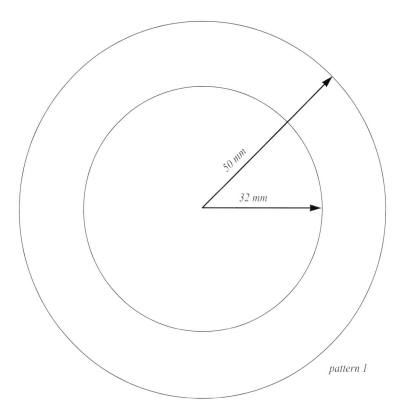

50 mm

32 mm

*pattern 1*

13

# 6. POSITIONING

In our first exercise we printed the stamp more or less in the centre of a sheet of parchment paper. In many cases we will want to print the stamp at an exact location. Let's see how that is done.
Measuring with the help of the stamp block may not be good enough, because the rubber part of the stamp may not be positioned exactly in line.
To make a window hanging with pattern no. 2, the stamp used is PS1: "Flowers in Leaded Glass" one must position the stamp in exactly the right spot. To achieve setting the stamp in the exact position required, we use the Pergamano® ruler and a parchment paper stencil we made ourselves (6.1).

## 6.1 Making a stencil

- take a piece of parchment paper of about 10 x 10 cm. (it should be big enough for the stamp) with at least one original right angle
- place the piece of parchment paper in such a way that the right angle will be at the bottom left corner, and mark a cross in that corner
- affix the stencil to the surface with 2 strips of adhesive tape
- put transparent or, even better, dark coloured stamping ink on the stamp.

## 6.2 Ruler for stamping

- Place the right angle of the ruler right alongside the bottom left side of the stencil. Take care that

both the long side and the short side of the ruler are against the sides of the stencil
- hold the stamp in the proper position for making a print and mark a small cross on the left bottom side of the stamp (the cross mark on the stencil and on the stamp will from now on determine the exact position of the stamp)
- hold the ruler firmly in place with one hand, but now remove the stencil.
- now make a print by pressing the stamp in to the corner of the ruler with the other hand. The stamp should touch the ruler at the bottom and side
- remove the stamp (picture 8)
- the stencil is now ready. Keep this stencil, it will be of use when you want to position or combine this stamp again. This stencil can only be used for this particular stamp: if you take another

*8*

stamp with the same pattern (or pattern number) the rubber stamp part may not be affixed in the exact same place.

## 6.3 Working with the stamping ruler

We will now continue with project no. 2. We start with making a print of stamp PS1 exactly in the middle of the pattern. Centre on the cross. Work as follows:

- make a photocopy of pattern no. 2 on page 22 (window hanging)
- place a sheet of parchment paper on the pattern
- affix it with 2 pieces of adhesive tape
- centre the stencil on the stamping mark
- hold it in position with one hand
- position the ruler alongside the bottom left of the stencil; take care that the ruler touches the stencil at both sides and that the ruler does not move (picture 9). The cross on the stamp should be against the cross marked on the stencil
- hold the ruler in place with one hand and remove the stencil

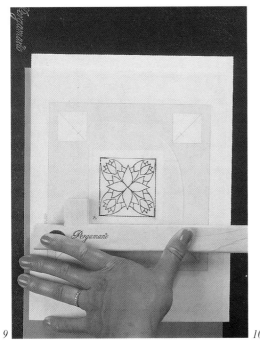

*9*

*10*

- make a print by pressing the stamp in to the corner of the ruler with the other hand (picture 10).

It will take a bit of practise and skill to hold the stamp ruler in position with the one hand and make a print with the other.
Now sprinkle the embossing powder on to the wet print and heat until it melts. You will see the result on picture 11.

You are now familiar with the use of the ruler. From now on you are able to make beautiful stamp prints anywhere you want with the use of this ruler and the stencil.

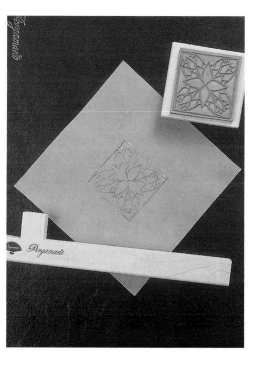

# 7. DIVIDING AND COMBINING

## 7.1 Dividing

Apart from making a complete print of a stamp, we can also print only part of a stamp pattern. This opens the door to a whole new range of opportunities. We can use parts of a stamp pattern separately or add parts to an original stamp print.

### Printing part of a stamp

We will take Perga-Stamp PS 1 and make a print of a small part (the flower part) in the corners of the piece of work with the same stamp.
This is how it is done:

1. moisten just that small part of the stamp pattern with a felt tip pen (see picture 12)
2. print the stamp where you want it with the help of the ruler and stencil
3. sprinkle embossing powder on to the still wet print
4. melt the embossing powder.

Moisten the desired part of the stamp pattern with a light coloured Perga-Color felt tip pen. Take a felt tip pen that still has enough ink or use a special (colourless) felt tip pen to moisten part of the stamp (picture 12). You can buy these felt tip pens in shops where you can buy creative rubber stamping materials.

Apply the ink carefully to the part of the stamp you want to print: the flower part.

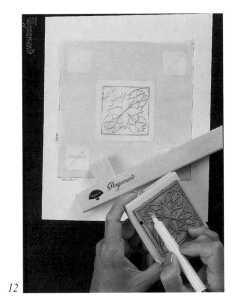

*12*

Centre the stencil of your stamp in such a way on your project that the flower part will be on the indicated spot (picture 13); in this case on the mark in one of the 4 corners of the project. Make a print with the help of the ruler for stamping.

### Block out stencil

There is a second way of printing the flower part of the stamp pattern: by using a home-made 'block out' stencil.

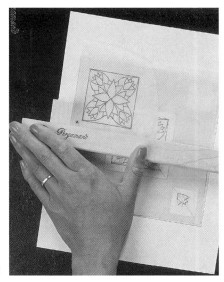

13

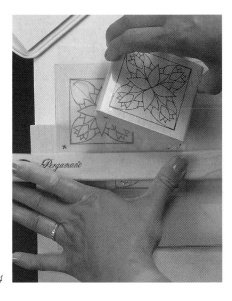

14

- make a dark coloured print of the whole stamp pattern on a separate piece of parchment paper; mark a cross at the bottom left of the stencil.
- carefully cut the flower part you want to print out of the stencil
- place the cut out flower part where you want to print it
- hold this little piece of stencil in place while you add the rest of the stencil, forming one whole stencil again
- now hold the rest of the stencil in place while you remove the little flower part
- affix the rest of the stencil to the project with adhesive tape
- position the ruler for stamping

- moisten the stamp with transparent ink from the ink pad (the whole stamp or just the flower part you want)
- make a print (picture 14)
- sprinkle embossing powder on to the print
- melt the embossing powder
- repeat this exercise 3 times for the other 3 corners.

You can see the result of this exercise on picture 15.

## 7.2 Combining

Besides the stamping of parts of the stamp pattern, we can also enlarge a stamp print by adding parts of the same stamp or of another stamp.

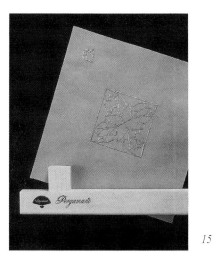

*15*

### Even more ideas:
Pergamano⁸ leaded glass window stamps offer even more ingenious ideas:
- by using just parts of the stamp pattern
- by adding parts of a stamp pattern to the whole stamp pattern
- you can emboss, perforate, cut and stipple inside the stamp pattern
- you can make certain parts of the stamp pattern in 3-D technique
- you can colour the stamp pattern in various ways with various colouring materials
- and.... you can combine the stamps with other materials, for example coloured cardboard passe-partouts.

Through dividing and combining, you can create a lot of variety with your projects, just using one Perga-Stamp. You will find an example of this on the cover of this booklet: the straight lines of the pattern have been left out and the heart shapes have been added 4 times.

## Tips
- Breathe against the stamp before you make a print. This will lead to a better print.
  Use a cotton cloth and a drop of detergent to remove grease marks e.g. fingerprints, from the parchment paper
- Do not hang your creation in direct sunlight for the colours will fade rather quickly
- To obtain really bright colours, you could colour on both the front and reverse side of the parchment paper
- Use Tinta silver ink and a mapping pen to touch up missing parts of a line.
- It is better to glue your passe-partout parts together with thin double-sided adhesive tape rather than with glue.

# 8. MORE PIECES OF WORK

On the basis of the techniques you have now learned, you will also be able to make the other pieces of work that are shown in the pictures.

*Pattern 2*
*Enlarge by 154% on a photocopier*

You will find all the necessary patterns in this booklet.

### Picture on the front cover

• Window hanging (Perga-Stamp PS4, pattern 2) This project is made the same way as project 2 (page 14). Note the fact that the straight outlines of the stamp print has been left out.

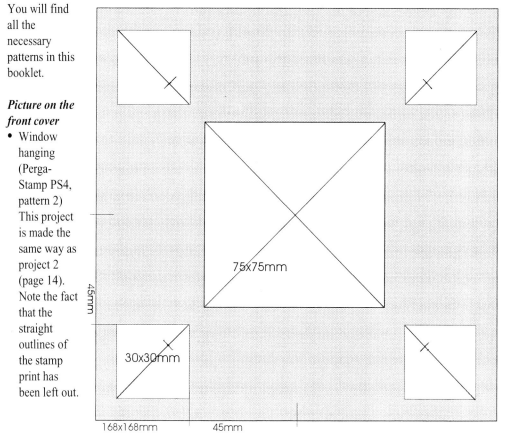

75x75mm

45mm

30x30mm

168x168mm

45mm

———— cut
- - - - - emboss at the back
-··-··- emboss at the front

- Window hanging (stamp PS1, pattern 2). In the chapter 'Stamping' you will find the working instruction for this project.
- Large box (stamp PS1, pattern 3). Enlarge the pattern on page 24 by 167% on a photocopier for the lid part.
  Photocopy again by157% for the box part. This latter part does not have decorations on the sides.

- Small box (Perga-Stamp PS4, pattern 3, see also large box on page 26).
  Photocopy the pattern by 125% for the cover part. Copy the pattern again, enlarged by 117 %, for the box part.
  Decorate the sides of the lid with perforations, cuttings and embossing to your own creative ideas and taste.
- Gift label (Perga-Stamp PS2, pattern 4).
  No special instructions are required here as the pattern and the picture show clearly how the label has been made.

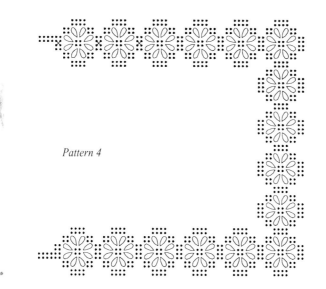

*Pattern 4*

### Picture on page 11
- Apperture cards (Perga-Stamp PS4, pattern 5 and 6).
- Gift label (Perga-Stamp PS4, pattern 7).

### Picture on page 15
- Large box (Perga-Stamp PS4, pattern 3). This box is basically the same as the little one on page 25.
- Shown is also the project from the chapter 'Stamping' and the piece of work the mobile (Perga-Stamp PS2, pattern 1).

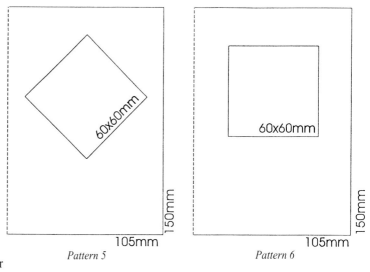

*Pattern 5*

*Pattern 6*

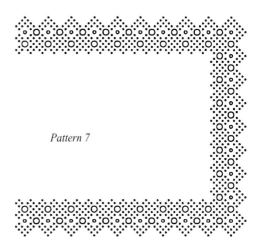

*Pattern 7*

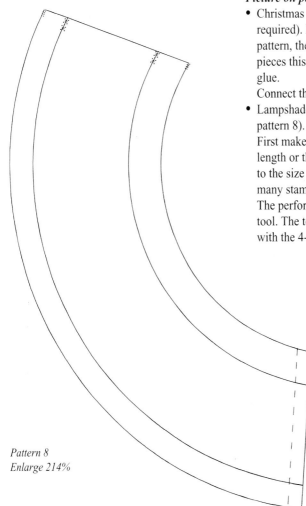

### *Picture on page 19*

- Christmas mobile (Perga-Stamp PS3, pattern not required). First emboss, then stipple the crystal pattern, then perforate it and cut it out. Make 6 pieces this way and affix them together with glue.
  Connect the mobile pieces with sewing thread.
- Lampshade on a wine glass (Perga-Stamp PS3, pattern 8).
  First make a copy of the template and adjust the length or the enlargement percentage according to the size of your wine glass. Find out how many stamp prints will fit on the template. The perforations are made with the 5-needle tool. The top and bottom outlines are perforated with the 4-needle tool and cut out.

*Pattern 8*
*Enlarge 214%*

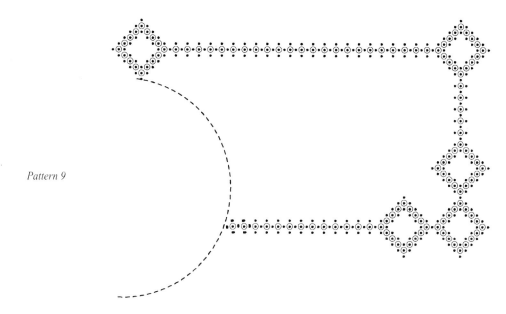

*Pattern 9*

**Picture on page 23**
- Label (Perga-Stamp PS2, pattern 9).
  Glue your piece of work on to cardboard label.
- The decorations on the other labels are made
  with parts of the stamp print.

**Picture on page 27**
- Christmas card (Perga-Stamp PS3, pattern 10).
  The crystal pattern will stand out best when
  stippled.
  The pattern and the picture show how it is done.

*Pattern 10*

30

## Picture on page 31

- Bag (stamp PS4, pattern 11).
  Perforate the flower petals in the centre and bend them outwards.
  Mount an identical extra flower on top as a 3-D element.
  Mount the petals overlapping.

*Pattern 11*
*Enlarge 164%.*

32

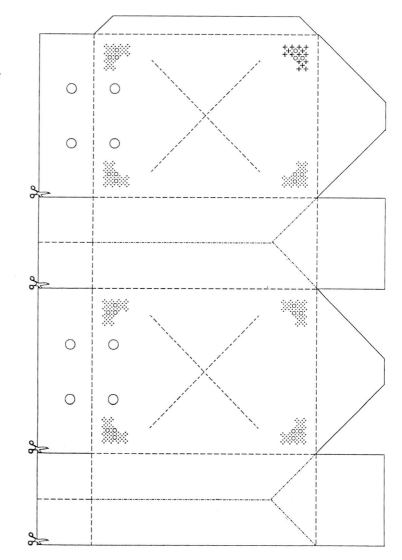